Country ABCs

Canada ABCs

A Book About the People and Places of Canada

Written by Brenda Haugen • Illustrated by David Shaw

Special thanks to our advisers for their expertise:
David Jay Bercuson, Ph.D.
Professor of History
University of Calgary, Alberta, Canada

Susan Kesselring, M.A., Literacy Educator
Rosemount-Apple Valley-Eagan (Minnesota) School District

PICTURE WINDOW BOOKS
Minneapolis, Minnesota

*For my treasured Canadian friends, especially Marianne, Ryan, Justin, and Jayme.
You meet the most amazing people in Grand Forks! And a special thanks to Bob,
my mentor and friend, for allowing me this and many, many other opportunities. —B.H.*

*The author wishes to thank Carol Puri, Ryan Bridge, Steve Hawkins, Marianne Cassels,
and Chris Ward for their time and expertise. I wouldn't have wanted to do it without you!*

Managing Editor: Bob Temple
Creative Director: Terri Foley
Editor: Nadia Higgins
Editorial Adviser: Andrea Cascardi
Copy Editor: Laurie Kahn
Designer: John Moldstad
Page production: Picture Window Books
The illustrations in this book were prepared digitally.

Picture Window Books
5115 Excelsior Boulevard
Suite 232
Minneapolis, MN 55416
1-877-845-8392
www.picturewindowbooks.com

Printed in the United States of America.

Library of Congress Cataloging-in-Publication Data
Haugen, Brenda.
Canada ABCs : a book about the people and places of Canada /
written by Brenda Haugen ; illustrated by David Shaw.
p. cm. — (Country ABCs)
Summary: An alphabetical exploration of the people, geography, animals, plants,
history, and culture of Canada. Includes bibliographical references and index.
ISBN 978-1-4048-0285-8 (hardcover)
ISBN 978-1-4048-0361-9 (paperback)
1. Canada—Juvenile literature. 2. English language—Alphabet—
Juvenile literature. [1. Canada. 2. Alphabet. 3. Canada. 4. Alphabet.]
I. Shaw, David, ill. II. Title. III. Series.
F1008.2 .H38 2004
971—dc22
2003016660

Hello! That's how Canadians greet one another in English.

Bonjour! (bohn-JOOR) And that is how they greet one another in French, Canada's second official language.

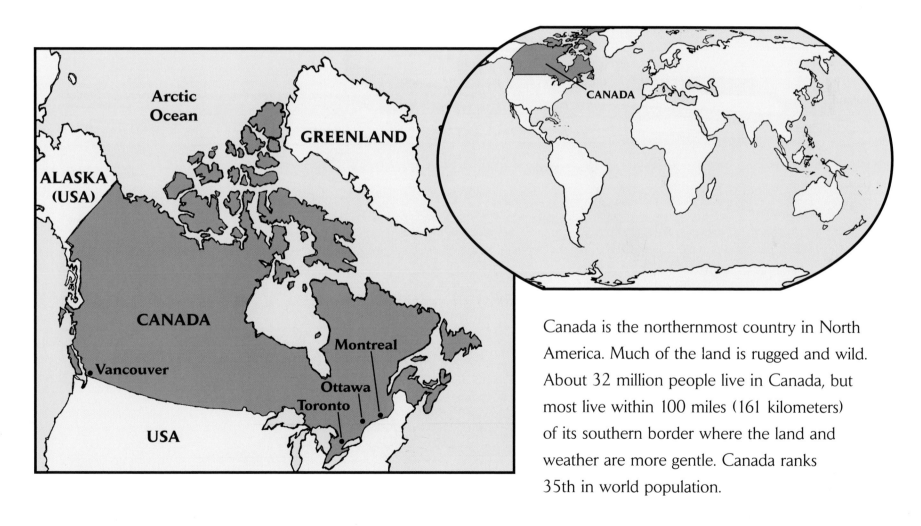

Canada is the northernmost country in North America. Much of the land is rugged and wild. About 32 million people live in Canada, but most live within 100 miles (161 kilometers) of its southern border where the land and weather are more gentle. Canada ranks 35th in world population.

A is for the Arctic Ocean.

Canada touches three oceans—the Arctic, the Atlantic, and the Pacific. If you add up all of the country's land that touches an ocean, Canada has the longest coastline of any nation in the world.

FAST FACT: Canada is the second largest country on earth. Only Russia is bigger.

B is for beaver.

The beaver is a Canadian national symbol. Europeans came to Canada in search of valuable fur long before Canada was its own country. Beaver furs, or pelts, were worth the most and could even be used as money!

FAST FACT: *Bears, moose, deer, rabbits, geese, mountain goats, and elk all live in Canada. The Arctic region is home to walruses, musk oxen, seals, and whales.*

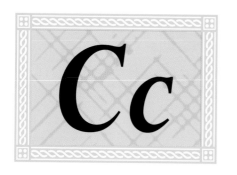

C is for comedians.

Some of the world's most famous comedians grew up in Canada. Jim Carrey is known for his goofy physical comedy and funny faces. Mike Myers is best known for his Austin Powers characters. He also was the voice of Shrek. Michael J. Fox starred in TV shows such as *Family Ties* and *Spin City*, as well as in the Back to the Future movies.

Jim Carrey

Mike Myers

Michael J. Fox

D is for dinosaur.

Scientists have found some of the most amazing dinosaur fossils in Canada. In Saskatchewan, they have found a nearly complete skeleton of a Tyrannosaurus rex. They also found a huge skeleton of a dinosaur that looked like a crocodile!

FAST FACT: One of the most famous dinosaur museums in the world, the Royal Tyrrell Museum of Paleontology, is found in Drumheller, Alberta. It is named after Joseph Burr Tyrrell, a Canadian scientist. Tyrrell found hundreds of dinosaur bones in Alberta during the late 1800s.

E is for **explorers**.

French and English explorers helped form the country of Canada. People from France were among the first Europeans to settle this land. England took control of the area from the French in the 1700s. England controlled Canada until 1931, when Canada gained its independence.

F is for flag.

Nearly half the land in Canada is covered with trees, so it's not surprising its flag has a leaf on it. The maple leaf has been a Canadian symbol for many years. Canada's flag design became official February 15, 1965.

FAST FACT: *Before the new flag was agreed upon, Canada flew the flag of the British colonies. Work to design Canada's new flag started in 1925.*

G is for gold rush.

The richest gold find in the world was discovered in the Klondike region of the Yukon Territory in 1896. More than a billion dollars in gold was mined during the Klondike gold rush. Though the area was cold and dangerous, more than 100,000 people flocked to the Klondike in hopes of becoming rich.

FAST FACT: Mounties made sure laws were followed during the Canadian gold rush. Known by their red coats and beautiful horses, the Mounties brought law and order to the Canadian frontier. They now are called the Royal Canadian Mounted Police.

Hh

H is for hockey.

Hockey is the most popular sport in Canada. Canada is home to some of the best players of all time, including Wayne Gretzky. Gretzky is the leading scorer in the history of the National Hockey League.

FAST FACT: Canada made history at the 2002 Olympics by earning gold medals in both men's and women's hockey. It was the first time one country had won both events.

I is for Inuit.

Once known as Eskimos, the Inuit people have lived in Canada for more than a thousand years. Many continue to live in the Arctic region of the country. About 2 percent of Canadians are Inuit or from other native cultures. The Inuit, Iroquois, Ojibwa, and Cree are among the groups native to Canada.

This *inukshuk* is a stone figure first built by the Inuit to serve as a landmark. People traveling along the main highway in Ontario can see thousands of inukshuk made by tourists and local citizens. The figures share the silent message with people who pass by: "We were here."

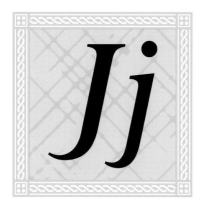

J is for Juno Awards.

The Juno Awards give special recognition to Canadian singers, songwriters, and musicians. Some of the most popular singers in the world are Canadian. Celine Dion and Shania Twain have sold millions of records. Both have earned many Juno Awards.

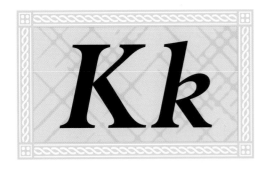

K is for kanata.

Canada's name comes from the Iroquois Indian word *kanata*. Kanata means "community" or "village." When French explorer Jacques Cartier first heard Indians use the word *kanata*, he thought they were saying Canada. He believed that was what they called the country. The name stuck!

L is for loonie.

Loonie is a nickname for a Canadian dollar. It is a bronze-plated coin with a picture of a loon on it. One hundred pennies make one loonie, or dollar. Canadians also have a toonie, a silver-and-gold-colored coin that is worth two dollars. Other coins include the nickel, dime, and quarter. Paper money comes in $5, $10, $20, $50, $100, and $1,000 bills.

FAST FACT: Pictures of Great Britain's Queen Elizabeth II are found on all Canadian coins and some bills. The queen plays a symbolic role in Canada's government, but she has no real power.

M is for maple syrup.

The sap from maple trees is used to make maple syrup, a favorite treat in Canada. Canadians pour maple syrup on pancakes, waffles, and French toast. Maple also is used to flavor candies, ice cream, cookies, and other goodies.

FAST FACT: *Canadian food and American food have a few differences. Many Canadians dip french fries in vinegar. And salt-and-vinegar potato chips are a favorite treat.*

N is for Nellie McClung.

To those who supported her, Nellie McClung was known as Our Nell. Nellie was a writer and teacher who helped get Canadian women the right to vote. She was one of the Famous Five, a group of women who battled in Canada's courts and government. They wanted Canadian law to say that women should have the same freedoms as men.

FAST FACT: In 1916, Manitoba became the first province to allow women to vote and run for public office. Nellie had lived in Winnipeg, Manitoba, and the small town of Manitou, Manitoba, for many years.

O is for Ottawa.

Oo

Ottawa, Ontario, is Canada's capital. Canada's laws are made in the Parliament buildings, known by their green roofs. The Parliament is made up of the Senate and the House of Commons. The head of Canada's government is the prime minister.

FAST FACT: *Each May, Ottawa hosts the Canadian Tulip Festival. The event started after the queen of the Netherlands sent tulip bulbs to Ottawa. She wanted to thank Canada for letting her live there during World War II and for helping to free her country.*

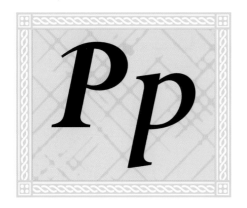

P is for provinces.

Canada is made up of 10 provinces and 3 territories. One province is named "Newfoundland and Labrador." It became Canada's newest province in 1949. Its rocky coasts are great for bird-watching.

FAST FACT: Each province and territory has its own local government. But territories are more closely governed by the federal government than the provinces are.

Q is for Quebec.

Quebec is Canada's largest province. Most of the people living in Quebec speak French. They are proud of their French culture. Montreal, Quebec, is the second largest city in Canada, after Toronto, Ontario.

FAST FACT: Nearly nine out of 10 people in Quebec are Roman Catholic. Canada as a whole is almost half Roman Catholic. The other half is made up mostly of Protestants who belong to the United Church of Canada.

R is for Rocky Mountains.

The Canadian Rocky Mountains form the largest mountain parkland in the world. Four parks—Banff, Jasper, Kootenay, and Yoho—lie right next to one another. Together they form one giant outdoor adventure area. People travel here to hike, mountain climb, ski, and enjoy the beautiful scenery.

FAST FACT: Glacier National Park in the Canadian Rockies has more than 400 glaciers. Glaciers are huge sheets of ice that form at the tops of mountains.

S is for the Stampede.

Each July, some of the world's toughest cowboys come to Canada for the Calgary Stampede. The 10-day event includes a rodeo, concerts, carnival rides, and lots of food. More than a million people take part in the fun during the Stampede.

T is for tuques (TEWKS).

In Canada, winter caps are called tuques. Canadians wear tuques during the very cold, snowy winter months. Some parts of Canada have the coldest weather in North America.

FAST FACT: Winter in most of Canada can be dangerous if you are not dressed properly. People dress in layers, including snow pants, parkas, boots, mittens, and tuques.

U is for Underground Railroad.

Many people of African descent found their way to Canada through the Underground Railroad. The Underground Railroad was a group of people that helped slaves escape from the United States to Canada in the 1800s. The former slaves were free when they arrived in Canada. Many of the relatives of these slaves chose to stay in Canada. The country is proud to offer equal opportunities to people of all races and continues to welcome immigrants from other countries.

V is for Vancouver.

Vancouver, British Columbia, is the busiest port in Canada. Ships can use the port at any time of year because the waters from Vancouver to the Pacific Ocean never freeze. Most of Canada's trade with Asia goes through this port.

FAST FACT: A statue of Terry Fox is one of Vancouver's famous sites. After losing his right leg to cancer, Fox tried to run all the way across Canada using an artificial leg. He got about halfway before he died of cancer, but he inspired many, many people.

25

W is for wheat.

Farmers grow enough wheat, barley, corn, and other produce to feed all of Canada—and still have a lot to sell to other countries. Fishing is another important industry, especially on the east and west coasts and in the Great Lakes area.

X is for XY Company.

The XY Company was one of the groups to set up trading posts in the northwest area of what is now Canada. The fur trade and the people it brought led to the birth of the country.

Fur traders often traveled west along Canada's many rivers.

Y is for
Yellowhead Highway.

The Yellowhead Highway is part of a roadway that stretches through the country's four westernmost provinces. It joins the Trans-Canada Highway in Manitoba. The Trans-Canada Highway is the world's longest national highway.

FAST FACT: *The St. Lawrence Seaway is another important transportation route in Canada. Since it opened in 1959, it has been the route ships use to reach central Canada from the Atlantic Ocean.*

Z is for zinc.

Zz

Canada is rich in natural resources and mines many minerals, including zinc, iron ore, and nickel. New Brunswick leads the country in zinc mining. Newfoundland and Labrador produces the most iron ore. And Ontario mines a great deal of the world's nickel.

FAST FACT: Canada's many forests produce wood for lumber and paper products. Oil, natural gas, and coal supply power for Canada and the countries with which it trades.

Canada in Brief

Official name: Canada

Capital: Ottawa (774,072 people)

Official languages: English and French

Population: 32 million

People: 66% European origin; 2% native Canadian; 6% Asian, African, or Arab; 26% mixed background

Religion: 46% Roman Catholic; 36% Protestant; 18% Jewish, Muslim, Buddhist, and other groups

Education: Public education is free for all children from kindergarten through 12th grade; most provinces require students to go to school for at least 10 years.

Major holidays: New Year's Day (January 1); Victoria Day (May); Canada Day (July 1); Labour Day (first Monday in September); Thanksgiving Day (second Monday in October); Christmas (December 25); Boxing Day (December 26)

Climate: In the south, the weather is mostly warm in summer and cold in winter with lots of snow. The weather is milder along the west coast and arctic in the north.

Area: 3,851,810 square miles (9,976,140 square kilometers) — a little larger than the United States

Highest point: Mount Logan, 19,550 feet (5,959 meters)

Lowest point: Atlantic and Pacific oceans, sea level

Type of government: confederation with parliamentary democracy

Head of government: prime minister

Major industries: fishing, forestry, mining, and manufacturing

Natural resources: precious metals, fish, timber, wildlife, coal, petroleum, natural gas, hydropower

Major agricultural products: wheat, barley, oilseed, tobacco, fruits, vegetables, dairy products, forest products

Chief exports: motor vehicles and parts, wood pulp, timber, crude petroleum, natural gas, electricity, wheat

Money: Canadian dollar

Say It in French

good-bye . . . . *adieu* (a-DEW)

good evening . . . . *bonsoir* (bohn-SWAH)

food . . . . *cuisine* (kwi-ZEEN)

thank you . . . . *merci* (mair-SEE)

no . . . . *non* (NOH)

yes . . . . *oui* (WEE)

please . . . . *s'il vous plait* (SEE VOO PLAY)

Glossary

fossils—remains of plants or animals that lived long ago

glacier—a large sheet of ice that forms at the top of a mountain

hockey—a game played by two teams that skate on ice. Players use long sticks to try to shoot a flat, circular puck into the other team's goal, or net.

seaway—a water route that ships can follow

vinegar—a sour liquid, often made from cider, that is used to give food flavor

To Learn More

More Books to Read

Auch, Alison. *Welcome to Canada*. Minneapolis, Minn.: Compass Point Books, 2003.

Frost, Helen. *A Look at Canada*. Mankato, Minn.: Pebble Books, 2002.

Kalman, Bobbie, and Niki Walker. *Canada From A to Z*. New York: Crabtree Pub. Co., 1999.

Rogers, Barbara Radcliffe, and Stillman D. Rogers. *Canada*. New York: Children's Press, 2000.

On the Web

FactHound offers a safe, fun way to find Web sites related to topics in this book. All of the sites on FactHound have been researched by our staff.

1. Visit *www.facthound.com*
2. Type in this special code: 1404802851
3. Click on the FETCH IT button.

Your trusty FactHound will fetch the best sites for you!

Index